LATER ELEMENTARY

TAKE A BOW!

8 SPARKLING PIANO SOLOS

BOOK 3

BY CAROLYN MILLER

T0079547

ISBN 978-1-61774-268-2

WILLIS MUSIC

EXCLUSIVELY DISTRIBUTED BY

HAL•LEONARD® CORPORATION
7777 W. BLUEMOUND RD. P.O. BOX 13819 MILWAUKEE, WI 53213

Visit Hal Leonard Online at
www.halleonard.com

FROM THE COMPOSER

Recital time should be a happy time! I believe that the recital solo should be carefully chosen to give each student the best chance for success in front of an unfamiliar audience. It is my hope that students will master the carefully selected solos in this book so that a winning performance takes place.

Book 3 contains some of my most favorite recital and teaching solos. "Mist" gives the student a chance to play a singing melody entwined with graceful arpeggios. "Crossover" is patterned but moves quickly, and, as the title suggests, is full of impressive hand-crossings. "Fireflies" is a flashy piece that my students always love to play. (This was the piece Regis Philbin once played on his nationally televised show—very exciting for me!) Lastly—in my opinion—all of the solos in this book sound more difficult than they really are. So, practice hard, enjoy your performances, and aim to impress!

My wish is that these pieces will entertain as well as motivate students of any age.

Please enjoy!

Carolyn Miller

CONTENTS

Mist

Carolyn Miller

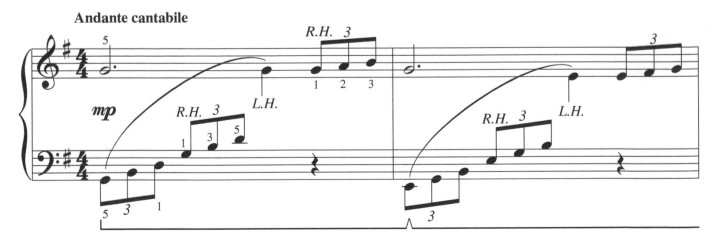

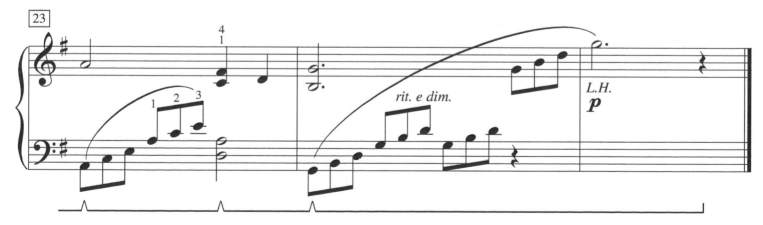

Crossover

Carolyn Miller

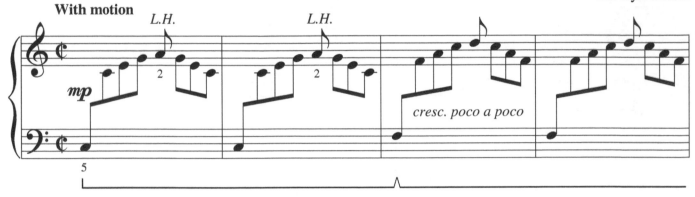

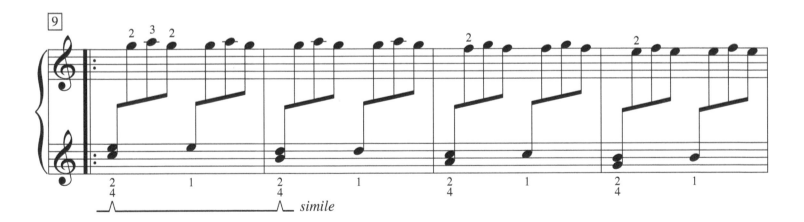

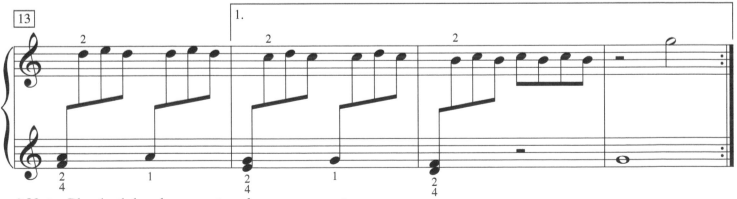

* **Note**: Play both hands one octave lower on repeat.

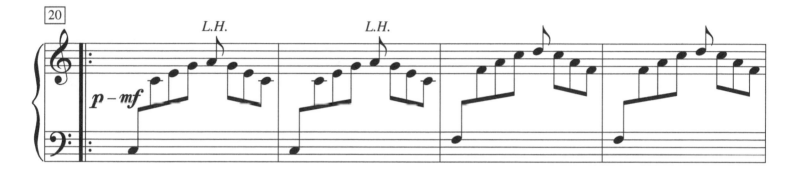

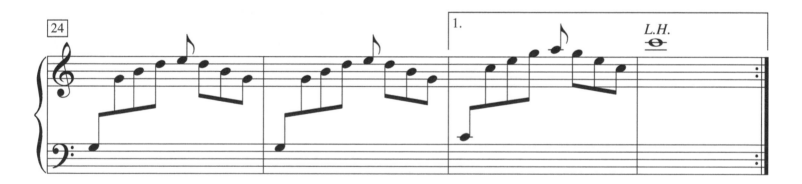

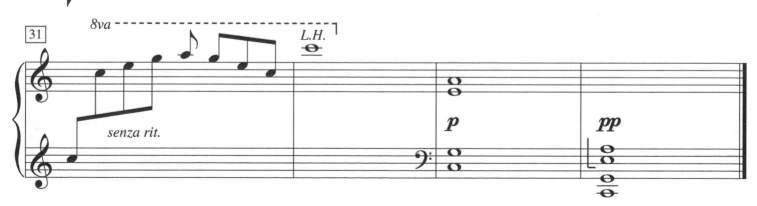

Cat and Mouse

Carolyn Miller

Fireflies

Carolyn Miller

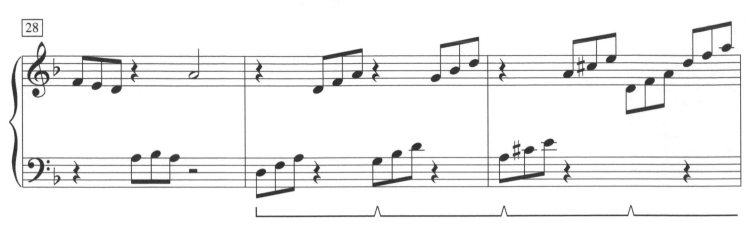

Arabian Dance

Carolyn Miller

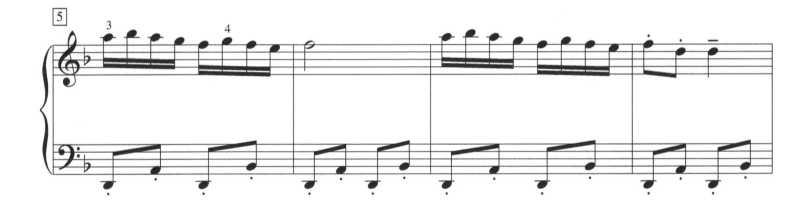

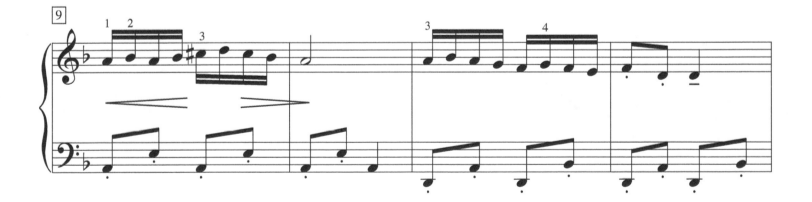

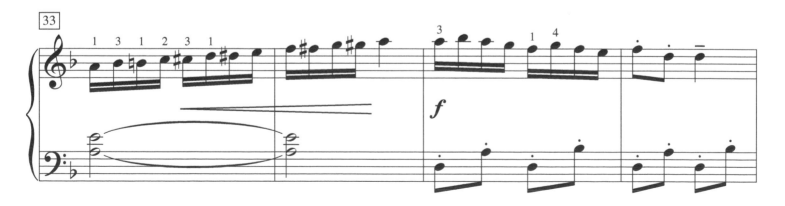

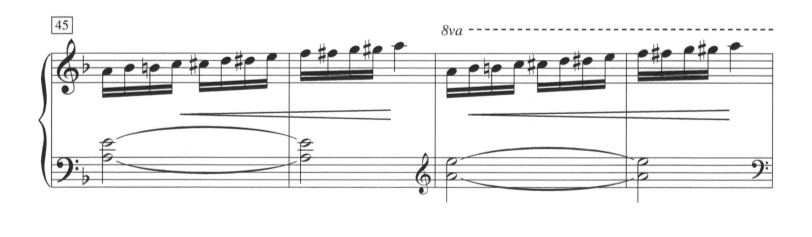

To the students of Music Rockwall

Spanish Dance

Carolyn Miller

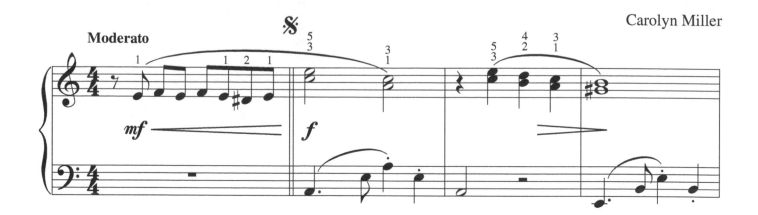

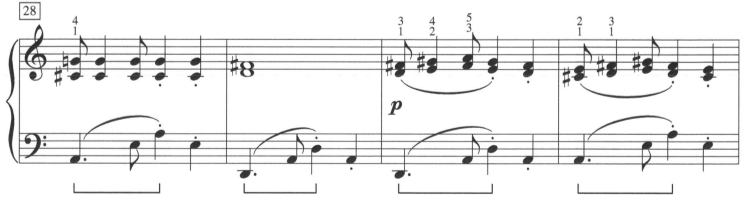

D.S. al Coda

CODA

The Busy Bee

Carolyn Miller

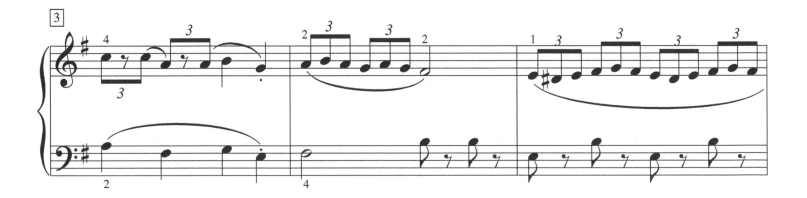

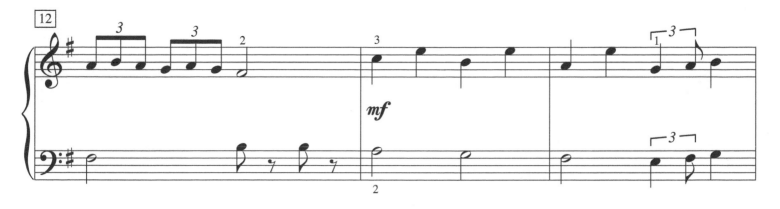

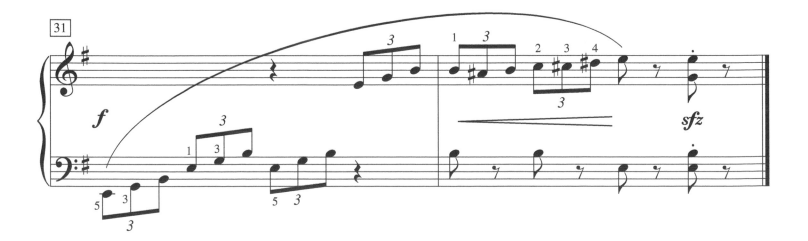

Flight of the Fly

Carolyn Miller

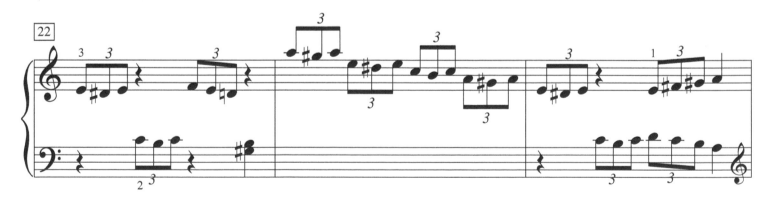

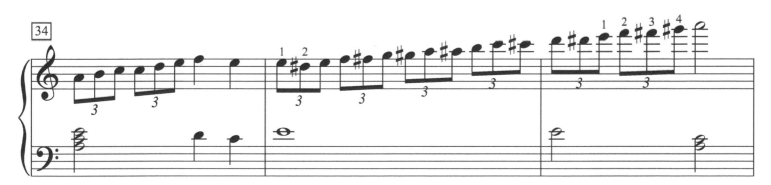

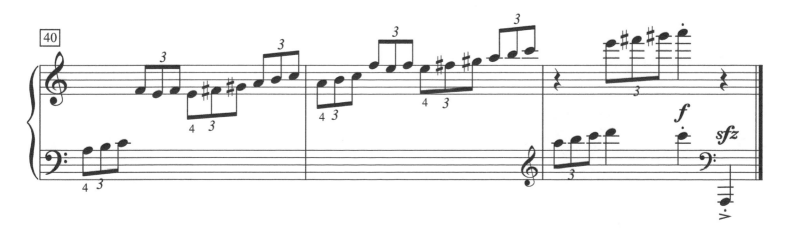

ABOUT THE COMPOSER

Carolyn Miller's teaching and composing career spans over 40 prolific years. She graduated with honors from the College Conservatory of Music at the University of Cincinnati with a degree in music education, and later earned a masters degree in elementary education from Xavier University. Carolyn regularly presents workshops throughout the United States and is a frequent adjudicator at festivals and competitions. Although she recently retired from the Cincinnati public school system, she continues to maintain her own private studio.

Carolyn's music emphasizes essential technical skills, is remarkably fun to play, and appeals to both children and adults. Well-known television personality Regis Philbin performed her pieces "Rolling River" and "Fireflies" in 1992 and 1993 on national television. Carolyn's compositions appear frequently on state contest lists, including the NFMC Festivals Bulletin. She is listed in the *Who's Who in America* and *Who's Who of American Women*.

In her spare time Carolyn directs the Northminster Presbyterian Church Choir in Cincinnati, Ohio and enjoys spending time with her family, especially her seven grandchildren.